I Like the Farm

Shelley Rotner

I Like to Read®

HOLIDAY HOUSE • NEW YORK

I Like to Read® books, created by award-winning picture book artists as well as talented newcomers, instill confidence and the joy of reading in new readers.

We want to hear every new reader say, "I like to read!"

Visit our website for flashcards and activities:
www.holidayhouse.com/I-Like-to-Read/
#ILTR
This book has been tested by an educational expert
and determined to be a guided reading level A.

To Charlie girl!

I like the cat.

I like the kitten.

I like the cow.

I like the calf.

I like the dog.

I like the pup.

I like the pig.

I like the piglet.

I like the hen.

I like the chick.

I like the farm.